THE
TOTALLY BAGEL
COOKBOOK

THE TOTALLY BAGEL COOKBOOK

by *Helene Siegel*

Illustrated by Carolyn Vibbert

CELESTIAL ARTS
BERKELEY, CALIFORNIA

The Totally Bagel Cookbook is produced by becker&mayer!, Ltd.

Printed in Singapore.

Cover design and illustration: Bob Greisen
Interior design and typesetting: Susan Hernday
Interior illustrations: Carolyn Vibbert

Library of Congress Cataloging-in-Publication Data
Siegel, Helene.
Totally Bagel / Helene Siegel.
    p.   cm.
ISBN 0-89087-832-3
1. Bagels   2. Cookery (Bagels)   I. Title.
TX770.B35S54   1997
641.8'15—dc21   97-1075
                                     CIP

Celestial Arts Publishing
P.O. Box 7123
Berkeley, CA 94707

Look for all 24 *Totally* books at your local store!

THANKS TO IZZY COHEN, FOR SHARING
HIS BAGEL RECIPE AND HIS WISDOM.

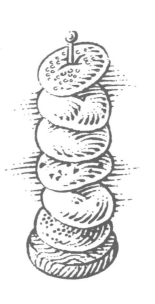

CONTENTS

INTRODUCTION

Given the bagel's intrinsic characteristics, what's not to like?

Bagels are chewy, inexpensive, and round. They are delicious for munching plain like a pretzel, for eating slathered with butter, cream cheese, or your favorite spread—or for a trip to nirvana—with cream cheese and lox.

Bagels appeal to health-conscious eaters for their low-fat, high-carbohydrate profile, and they appeal to mere pleasure seekers because they are deliciously satisfying. In addition, bagels make excellent, easy-to-hold teething rings, thanks to that hole in the center.

This is an auspicious moment in the history of the bagel. After several fits and starts—an upswing after the Jewish-Polish migration to New York during the first part of this century, a push from nationally distributed Lender's in the '60s—bagels seem to be finally working their way into the American culinary mainstream. Like pizza and tacos, which also started out as immigrant foods in this country, bagels are on that circuitous path of assimilation that takes a beloved foodstuff from one culture and puffs it up, crisps it up, sweetens it, or covers it with sauce, so that eventually it becomes something new—something beloved by an even larger audience of hungry eaters.

Where the homely bagel will end up is anybody's guess. Will the soft 5-ounce bagel become the norm? Are cinnamon-raisin bagels here to stay? Will tofu ever replace real cream cheese? Will bagels be just another baguette—a wonderful ethnic bread but not a daily part of the American diet? Or, even worse, are bagels a culinary fad, destined to oblivion like yesterday's kiwi?

As a dyed-in-the-wool bagel eater—I grew up on them in New York—my hunch is that they are here to stay. A bread of such strong character and dependability, around which you can build a small meal, is just too good a thing to pass up. So here are some good ideas—mostly solid, some silly—for enjoying your bagels while they are still hot.

FRESH BAGELS
AND
DAY-OLD USES

IZZY'S BAGELS

When it comes to making bagels at home, nobody said it would be easy. This authentic recipe comes from retired Los Angeles baker Izzy Cohen—who also helped Nancy Silverton at La Brea Bakery develop her specialty Jewish breads.

As far as Izzy is concerned, if it is worth doing something, it is worth doing it right. And he has seen a lot of wrong bagel recipes in his day. To Izzy, a bagel must be chewy. "I am a firm believer that foods that take chewing develop flavor in the chewing."

So read the recipe first and don't finagle any shortcuts. Keep in mind Izzy's words: You have only one (OK, maybe two or three) customer to please, and nothing compares with the satisfaction of making something yourself—especially something as wonderful and densely chewy as these handcrafted gems.

- 2 cups cool water
- 3 tablespoons sugar
- 1½ tablespoons salt
- 2 tablespoons barley malt syrup (available at health food stores)
- 7 cups bread flour, plus extra if the dough is sticky
- 1½ tablespoons dry milk
- 1½ tablespoons vital wheat gluten
- 5 teaspoons dry yeast
- cornmeal for dusting

In the bowl of a heavy-duty electric mixer with dough hook, place water, sugar, salt, and malt syrup. Mix to combine. In another bowl, mix together flour, dry milk, gluten, and dry yeast. Add to the liquid in the bowl all at once, and knead at low speed until dough clears the sides of the bowl. Continue kneading at low speed, until the dough is smooth, about 5 minutes. (If sticky, sprinkle in a bit more flour.)

Transfer to a board, cover with plastic wrap, and let rise 10 minutes. (Do not be concerned with a few wrinkles in the dough.)

With a dough blade or sharp knife, divide the dough into 16 pieces. On an unfloured board, knead each into a smooth ball. (First flatten with the palm of your hand, and then pull the edges into the center, bearing down and pushing away with the heel of your hand with each quarter-turn.) Cover with a towel, and let rest 5 minutes.

Have ready a cardboard sheet or wooden board, lightly dusted with cornmeal. To make the holes, pick up each ball and press a hole through the dough in the center with an index finger. Then push your other index finger through the opposing side, and pull and stretch the hole by running your fingers around each other, enlarging it to $1\frac{1}{2}$ to 2 inches. Place on coated sheets, cover with towel, and let rise $1\frac{1}{2}$ hours, until not quite doubled.

Meanwhile bring a large pot of water to a boil. Preheat oven to 425 degrees F, and get ready two sheet pans lined with parchment paper. (If you have baking or pizza tiles, place on the baking rack.)

Being careful not to crowd the pot, drop in three or four bagels at a time. (They should immediately rise to the surface.) Boil about 20 seconds, dunking and turning with a spoon to moisten evenly. Immediately transfer with slotted spoon to large strainer, being careful not to stack, and shake off excess liquid. If adding toppings, dip drained bagels in bowls of seeds or spices. Transfer to lined baking sheet.

Bake 15 to 20 minutes, turning once, until golden and crisp all over. Cool on racks, and store.

MAKES 16 3-OUNCE BAGELS

Toppings for dipping: sesame seeds, poppy seeds, and other seeds or mixtures such as caraway, sunflower, and fennel, to taste; coarse salt; dehydrated garlic chips; or a mixture of lightly sautéed minced garlic and chopped onions.

TIPS FROM IZ

- For a lighter, less chewy bagel, increase rising time.
- For a chewier bagel, increase boiling time.
- If bread flour is unavailable, use regular unbleached flour and double the gluten.
- Vital wheat gluten, the protein that adds elasticity to dough, is available in many supermarket baking sections.
- Add an additional tablespoon of sugar if dry milk is unavailable. The purpose of dry milk is to add color.

- If the holes close and the bagels puff when boiled, gently restretch and enlarge the hole just before boiling.
- The two identifying ingredients, without which your dough cannot bear the proud mantle of "bagel," are *malt syrup* for flavor and color and *gluten* for the extra chew.
- Once you master the novice method for punching bagel holes described here, you may want to graduate to the more time-honored method: Roll each piece by hand into a small log, and then roll each (with a rolling pin or possibly a pasta machine) into a 7-inch strip. Wrap the strip around your fingers at the knuckles to form a circle, overlapping about 1½ inch on the palm side. Roll the ends together on the counter until they form a seal.

Izzy Cohen's Bagel Treatment

So how does an 80-year-old maven like Izzy prefer to eat his morning bagel? First of all it should be plain—as far as Izzy is concerned, chocolate chips, raisins, and cinnamon are best left to cookies. He likes to toast his bagels whole, thereby improving the crust, then he splits them open and lightly coats them with butter and jam—preferably the tart, fruity quince preserves he makes himself. As a health-conscious eater, Izzy also points out that eating a 5-ounce bagel (the size of many bagel shop behemoths) is the equivalent in calories of eating five slices of bread.

BAGEL CROUTONS

Just the thing for a Jewish Caesar salad or plain chicken soup—bagel cubes drenched in butter and fried till crisp.

2 plain day-old bagels
3 tablespoons butter
2 garlic cloves, minced
1 tablespoon minced fresh herbs, such as
    thyme *or* parsley (optional)

With a good serrated knife, slice the bagels in half. Place cut-side down on a board and cut each into irregular ½-inch or smaller cubes.

Melt the butter with garlic and herbs, if desired, in a medium skillet over medium-high heat. Add bagel cubes, and quickly sauté just until crisp all over, 2 to 3 minutes. Cool, and store in zipper-lock bags.

MAKES 2 CUPS

HOMEMADE BAGEL CHIPS

With a food processor fitted with a slicing blade, old bagels can be converted to addictive, crunchy bagel chips in no time. (A countertop meat slicer may also be used.) Avoid bagels with toppings, as they may burn at high temperatures.

day-old plain bagels
olive oil for drizzling
chopped fresh thyme, oregano, *or* marjoram
salt, to taste

Preheat oven to 400 degrees F.

In a food processor fitted with a 4-mm slicing blade, place the bagels, one at a time, in the feed tube and slice vertically. Arrange chips in single layers on baking tray. Lightly drizzle with olive oil and sprinkle with herbs, if desired. Bake, checking and turning twice, until golden all over, 10 to 12 minutes. Lightly sprinkle with salt, and use plain for noshing, or with dips and spreads.

FRENCH TOAST À LA BAGEL

Consider this for breakfast emergencies—when nothing but French toast will do, and you are plum out of more appropriate breads.

2 day-old plain bagels
2 eggs
¼ cup milk
½ teaspoon cinnamon
¼ teaspoon ground nutmeg
1 to 2 tablespoons butter
2 tablespoons sugar mixed with ¼ teaspoon cinnamon *or* maple syrup for serving

Carefully slice the bagels in thirds, horizontally. In a shallow baking dish, beat together the eggs, milk, cinnamon, and nutmeg. Add the bagels, turning to coat evenly. Set aside 30 minutes to 1 hour.

To fry, melt the butter in a large skillet over medium heat. Add the bagels, and fry until golden brown and crisp on one side.

Turn, and cook until the second side is
brown and crisp. Serve hot with cinnamon
sugar or maple syrup.

SERVES 3

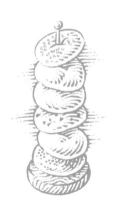

BAGEL AND LOX SALAD

Here is a new turn on an old combination:
bagels, cheese, and lox in a crisp, tart salad.

1 head romaine lettuce, washed, dried, and
    cut into bite-size pieces
½ cup soft goat cheese, crumbled
¼ cup tiny black olives such as pichoulines
    (or 2 tablespoons capers)
3 tablespoons red wine vinegar
1 teaspoon Dijon mustard
½ cup olive oil
salt and freshly ground black pepper
3 tablespoons chopped fresh herbs such as
    chives, parsley, *or* tarragon
1 recipe bagel croutons
3 ounces lox *or* smoked salmon, cut in
    thin strips

Place the lettuce in a serving bowl. Crumble on the goat cheese, add the olives, and toss.

In a small bowl, whisk together red wine vinegar, mustard, olive oil, salt, and pepper. Whisk in herbs. Pour over salad to coat lightly. Refrigerate any leftover dressing.

Sprinkle croutons and lox over salad. Lightly toss, and serve.

SERVES 4

SCHMEARS AND SPREADS

COUNTRY VEGETABLE SPREAD

This snappy, crunchy spread is my favorite thing, after cream cheese and lox, to put on a bagel. I remember it from Jewish dairy restaurants in my native New York.

1 (8-ounce) package cream cheese, softened
¼ cup sour cream
8 radishes, trimmed and diced
5 scallions, white and green, chopped
¼ cup diced red pepper
¼ cup diced celery
freshly ground black pepper
salt, to taste

Whip the cream cheese and sour cream with an electric mixer until light and fluffy. Add remaining ingredients, and gently beat just to combine. Keeps in the refrigerator about 5 days.

ENOUGH FOR 6 SERVINGS

LOX SPREAD

Lox ends, considered lower quality than the belly portion and less expensive, are sold at Jewish delis and some bagel stores. Just substitute regular lox, if ends are unavailable. Lox spread is a good use for leftover bits and pieces of smoked salmon.

1 (8-ounce) package cream cheese, softened
2 to 3 tablespoons heavy cream
3 ounces lox ends *or* trimmings, roughly chopped
1 teaspoon capers, drained
juice of ½ lemon
freshly ground black pepper

Whip the cream cheese and heavy cream with an electric mixer until light and fluffy. Add lox, capers, lemon, and pepper, and gently beat just to combine. Keeps in the refrigerator about 2 weeks.

ENOUGH FOR 6 SERVINGS

The New York Bagel

As the Neapolitan is to pizza, the New York bagel is the bagel against which all others must be measured, especially if you grew up on it. Its crust is glossy and browned, it cracks when you bite into it, and its inside is meant to fight back. Even to attempt to bite into a bagel older than one day is courting dental work. As for slicing it, consider yourself warned. Emergency rooms report a surge of bagel-related hand and finger injuries.

The original New York bagel was small, about 2 ounces, and came in two kinds: plain or egg. It was produced in little underground shops in Manhattan's Lower East Side, usually by a three-man team: one to mix the dough, one to kettle or boil, and one to bake. These bagels were sold as a street snack on sticks or strung on strings for sale in shops. Larger bagels, called "bulls," were specially made for restaurants and delicatessens. As they gained in popularity with the influx of Askenazic Jews from Europe, they may also have been produced by other general Jewish bakeries, though these would never be as good, since they were probably made with the dough left over from the night's bread-baking.

GARLIC AND ONION SPREAD

Use freshly minced garlic for the very best garlic flavor.

4 ounces softened goat cheese
4 ounces softened cream cheese
2 tablespoons heavy cream
1 garlic clove, minced
2 scallions, white and green, chopped
½ bunch chives, chopped
2 tablespoons chopped fresh Italian parsley
salt and freshly ground black pepper, to taste

Combine the goat cheese, cream cheese, and cream in the bowl of an electric mixer. Beat until light and fluffy. Add remaining ingredients, and gently beat until combined. Keeps in the refrigerator about 1 week.

ENOUGH FOR 6 TO 8 SERVINGS

FRESH STRAWBERRY CREAM CHEESE SPREAD

Homemade strawberry spread is a nice treat for summer brunch. Serve on pumpernickel or raisin bagels.

1 cup chopped, stemmed strawberries
1 tablespoon sugar
1 (8-ounce) package cream cheese, softened
2 tablespoons heavy cream
1 teaspoon vanilla

Combine the berries and sugar in a small bowl and let sit 5 minutes.

Whip the cream cheese, heavy cream, and vanilla in bowl of electric mixer until light and fluffy. Add sweetened berries, and gently mix just to combine. Keeps in the refrigerator 2 days.

ENOUGH FOR 6 SERVINGS

FIGGY CREAM CHEESE SPREAD

Try this rich spread on a sesame bagel. Chopped walnuts may be added for extra crunch.

1 (8-ounce) package cream cheese, softened
1 tablespoon heavy cream
1 tablespoon lemon juice
2 or 3 drops anise extract *or*
    ¼ teaspoon Pernod
½ cup chopped, dried figs

Whip the cream cheese, heavy cream, lemon juice, and anise extract or liqueur in the bowl of an electric mixer until light and fluffy. Add the figs, and beat to combine. Keeps in the refrigerator about 2 weeks.

ENOUGH FOR 6 SERVINGS

CRANBERRY PECAN SPREAD

*This tart, crunchy cheese spread also makes a
good dip for fresh vegetables.*

¾ cup pecan halves
1 teaspoon sugar
½ teaspoon cinnamon
pinch of ground nutmeg
1 (8-ounce) package cream cheese, softened
1 tablespoon heavy cream
½ tablespoon grated orange zest (optional)
¾ cup dried cranberries, chopped

Preheat oven to 350 degrees F. In a small bowl, mix together pecans, sugar, cinnamon, and nutmeg. Spread on baking sheet, and toast 15 minutes. Cool and chop.

Beat cream cheese, cream, and orange zest in the bowl of an electric mixer until light and fluffy. Add chopped nuts with spices and cranberries. Mix to combine. Keeps in the refrigerator about 2 weeks.

ENOUGH FOR 6 SERVINGS

How to Slice a Bagel

In the interest of reducing the caseloads at over-crowded emergency rooms, here is my foolproof method for cutting open a bagel. Using a serrated blade and holding the bagel in a towel-wrapped hand, cut the bagel in half by sawing back and forth. Stop when the bagel stops.

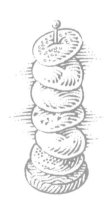

DATE WALNUT SPREAD

Try this wonderful spread on thinly sliced dark bread or a rye or pumpernickel bagel.

1 (8-ounce) package cream cheese, softened
1 tablespoon heavy cream
½ cup chopped, pitted dates
½ cup toasted walnuts, chopped in
   large chunks

Beat the cream cheese and cream in the bowl of an electric mixer until light and fluffy. Add the dates and walnuts, and mix in by hand. Keeps in the refrigerator about 1 week.

ENOUGH FOR 6 SERVINGS

RICOTTA WITH HONEY AND APPLES

Ricotta and apples make a fragrant morning spread for your toasted bagel. Because of its moisture from fresh apples, this delicate spread does not keep well. It is best served within a few hours.

1 cup ricotta cheese
1½ tablespoons honey
¾ cup diced, peeled apple such as Gala, Fuji, *or* Granny Smith
⅛ teaspoon cinnamon

In a bowl, with a fork, mix together the ricotta and honey. Add the apples and cinnamon, and gently mix to combine. Keeps about 1 day in the refrigerator.

ENOUGH FOR 2 SERVINGS

How to Shop for the Best Bagel

All bagels are, of course, good, by their very nature. However, if it is the best, or most authentic, you are searching for, look for a shop that sells only bagels, with perhaps a pack of cream cheese and lox in the refrigerator case—nothing weird or cutting edge. The older and simpler the shop, generally the better. If you have any Jewish friends in town, you can save yourself a headache and just ask them for a recommendation. Do not judge a book by its cover. Some of the best bagels in New York and Los Angeles are baked by non-Jews since the trade has been passed along to other ethnic groups.

GOAT CHEESE
SUN-DRIED TOMATO SPREAD

Serve this lusty spread on an afternoon or evening snack bagel—preferably garlic— or on a thinly sliced, toasted baguette for an hors d'oeuvre.

- 8 ounces softened goat cheese
- 6 tablespoons olive oil
- 3 tablespoons chopped sun-dried tomatoes packed in oil
- 1 teaspoon minced garlic
- ¼ teaspoon red chile flakes

In a bowl, with a fork, mix together goat cheese and oil. Add sun-dried tomatoes, garlic, and chile flakes, and combine with fork. Keeps in the refrigerator about 2 weeks.

ENOUGH FOR 6 SERVINGS

GOAT CHEESE
AND HERB SPREAD

*Marinating goat cheese with garlic and herbs is a
typically French thing to do. It can stay in the
refrigerator, covered with oil and herbs, as long
as 2 weeks. Delicious served open-faced with
thinly sliced tomato and red onion or as a sandwich with mashed avocado on the facing side.*

4 ounces softened goat cheese
olive oil to cover
1 garlic clove, peeled and crushed
1 teaspoon black peppercorns
about 10 sprigs fresh herbs, such as rose-
  mary, thyme, basil, oregano

Place the goat cheese in a small container or bowl. Pour on enough oil to cover, and add garlic, peppercorns, and herbs. Cover and marinate at room temperature 1 day.

Before serving, lift cheese out of marinade. Mash with a fork and spread on toasted bagels.

ENOUGH FOR 3 SERVINGS

The average plain American bagel weighs in at 4.5 ounces, or about 360 calories.

CURRIED CREAM CHEESE SPREAD

Try this exotic spread on rye, sesame, or plain bagels.

1 (8-ounce) package cream cheese, softened
2 tablespoons heavy cream
1/4 cup confectioners' sugar
2 tablespoons curry powder
1/3 cup golden raisins

In the bowl of an electric mixer, beat together cream cheese and cream until light and fluffy. Add remaining ingredients, and beat until combined.

ENOUGH FOR 6 SERVINGS

CHIPOTLE CREAM CHEESE SPREAD

Hints of chile and smoke lend an air of mystery to this unusual spread. Chipotles—or dried, smoked red jalapeños—are available in cans in the international section of the supermarket.

1 (8-ounce) package cream cheese, softened
2 tablespoons heavy cream
1 teaspoon chopped canned chipotle
juice of 1 lime

Combine the ingredients in the bowl of a food processor fitted with the metal blade. Process until smooth and fluffy. Serve with thinly sliced tomato, cilantro sprigs, and red onions as garnish.

ENOUGH FOR 6 SERVINGS

ROCKY ROAD SPREAD

A sweet spread when all you have in the house is plain bagels, a storm is raging outside, and a stubborn toddler (or two) is crying out for chocolate chip bagels. Rocky road on a plain bagel should satisfy any child's daily quotient for a chewy, crunchy, sweet (not-too-bad-for-you) snack.

1 (8-ounce) package cream cheese, softened
2 tablespoons heavy cream
¼ cup chopped walnuts
¼ cup chocolate chips
2 tablespoons white chocolate chips

In the bowl of an electric mixer, beat together cream cheese and cream until light and fluffy. Add nuts and chips, and beat to combine. Store in the refrigerator.

ENOUGH FOR 6 SERVINGS

MOSTLY FISH
SANDWICHES

CREAM CHEESE
AND LOX SANDWICH

It would be negligent to omit this—the sine qua non *of bagel sandwiches—though most of us need no instruction. Probably the first choice of those whose teeth were cut on bagels.*

2 or 3 bagels
cream cheese, preferably whipped
¼ pound thinly sliced lox *or* smoked salmon
thinly sliced red onion, tomato, capers,
    lemon wedges as garnish
freshly ground black pepper

Split bagels open, and lightly toast, if desired.

Generously slather or lightly coat, according to preference, both sides with cream cheese. Top each with a layer of lox, and garnish and season according to taste, for open-face. For closed sandwich, layer lox on one side and close.

MAKES 2 OR 3 SANDWICHES

First Came the Word
The derivation of the word "bagel" can be traced to its Eastern European roots in Jewish culture: from the Old High German beigel, *to modern German* beugel, *meaning a "round bread," or* bugel, *meaning a "twisted or curved bracelet," or* buegel, *meaning "stirrup," to the Yiddish* beygel. *The similar-sounding Russian bubliki is a round roll sold on strings.*

CHOPPED HERRING SANDWICH

A zingy chopped herring spread like this is sold in many Jewish delis or specialty bagel shops. Heaven for herring people, such as myself.

1 (6-ounce) jar herring fillets in wine sauce
2 tablespoons diced red onion
1 hard-boiled egg white, minced
freshly ground black pepper
2 bagels, toasted
thinly sliced red onion, tomato, and lettuce
    leaves

Transfer the herring, along with the onions that come in the herring jar, to the bowl of a food processor. Process until a chunky paste is formed, and transfer to a bowl. Add the diced onion and the egg white, and gently combine with a fork. Season with pepper, and serve open-faced with thinly sliced onion, tomato, and lettuce.

ENOUGH FOR 2 SANDWICHES

SALMON SALAD SANDWICH

*Take a break from tuna with this other
fish-from-a-can sandwich.*

1 (7.5-ounce) can Alaska red salmon,
    drained
2 tablespoons olive oil
1 tablespoon lemon juice
2 tablespoons diced red onion
2 tablespoons chopped Kalamata olives
    or tapenade (see page 77)
2 bagels, toasted
thinly sliced tomato and lettuce leaves

Transfer the salmon to a bowl, and remove
any large bones. Flake and mash with a fork.
Add oil, lemon juice, red onion, and olives,
and combine and mash to form a spread.
Make sandwiches as you wish on bagels with
suggested toppings. Store in the refrigerator.

ENOUGH FOR 2 SANDWICHES

SARDINE SANDWICH

*For the sardine and bagel lovers of the world—
an easy fish spread for sandwich-making.*

1 (3.75-ounce) tin sardines packed in oil
3 tablespoons diced red onion
1 ounce cream cheese
juice of 1 lemon
freshly ground black pepper
1 plain, poppy, *or* onion bagel
red onion and tomato slices

Lift the sardines from the can, draining
excess oil. Place in a bowl along with
remaining ingredients. Season generously
with pepper. Mash to a paste with a fork.
Serve, open-face, on toasted plain, poppy, or
onion bagel. Garnish with thinly sliced red
onion and tomato.

MAKES 1 SANDWICH

TUNA TAPENADE SANDWICH

*Tuna salad is one sandwich filling for which few
Americans need a recipe. However, since it was
one of my favorite childhood sandwiches, preferably on a sesame or plain bagel, I am including
this version for posterity. Feel free to make your
own favorite additions: Olives, celery, mustard,
and relish are some popular possibilities.*

1 (6-ounce) can tuna
¼ cup diced red onion *or* scallions
1 tablespoon mayonnaise
juice of ½ lemon
freshly ground black pepper
2 tablespoons chopped fresh Italian parsley
1 bagel, toasted
tapenade (see page 77) *or* mayonnaise
sliced tomato and lettuce leaves as garnish

Drain the tuna and place in a bowl. Add remaining ingredients, season to taste with pepper and lemon, and mash with a fork. Spread on bottom half of a plain, sesame, onion, or garlic bagel. Lightly coat top half with tapenade (or mayo), and garnish tuna with thinly sliced tomato and lettuce.

MAKES 1 SANDWICH

"...It was a Jewish Sunday morning tradition for the men to go out to buy bagels, cream cheese, and lox so their wives could sleep in on Sunday morning (in the tradition of non-Jewish men making their own trilogy of bacon, eggs, and pancakes).

> *—from* Jewish Cooking in America *by Joan Nathan*

SHRIMP SALAD SANDWICH

¾ pound cooked and peeled bay *or*
    small shrimp
2 tablespoons mayonnaise
1 tablespoon lemon juice
3 or 4 dashes Tabasco
freshly ground black pepper
1 celery rib, trimmed and diced
2 bagels, toasted
thinly sliced red onion, tomato, and
    lettuce leaves

Process ½ pound of the shrimp in a food processor until finely chopped. Add mayonnaise, lemon juice, Tabasco, and pepper. Pulse to combine. Transfer to a bowl.

Roughly chop the remaining shrimp, and add with celery to mixture. Stir to combine, adjust seasonings, and serve on sandwiches or salads. For a sandwich, spread shrimp salad on bottom half. Top with onion, tomato, and lettuce, and mayonnaise-coated top half. Store leftovers in the refrigerator.

MAKES 1 CUP, ENOUGH FOR 2 LARGE SANDWICHES

LOBSTER SALAD SANDWICH

Lobster makes a terrific salad for spreading on sandwiches or nibbling on lettuce leaves.

1 cup cold cooked lobster meat, roughly chopped
¼ cup diced celery
½ Granny Smith apple, peeled, cored, and chopped
3 tablespoons prepared mayonnaise
1 tablespoon lemon juice
1 tablespoon chopped fresh tarragon
salt and freshly ground black pepper
2 bagels, toasted
thinly sliced red onion, tomato, and lettuce leaves

Combine the lobster, celery, and apple in a bowl. Add the mayonnaise, lemon juice, tarragon, salt, and pepper; toss to coat evenly. Make sandwich using bagels, onion, tomato, and lettuce, as desired. Store leftovers in the refrigerator.

MAKES ENOUGH FOR 2 SANDWICHES OR SALADS

EGG SALAD SANDWICH

Egg salad can be a real treat when freshly made and spread on a delicious toasted and buttered bagel—or egg bread, rye, or white toast in emergencies.

4 hard-boiled eggs, cooled and peeled
¼ cup chopped red onion
3 tablespoons prepared mayonnaise
2 tablespoons chopped fresh tarragon *or* basil
salt and freshly ground black pepper
2 plain *or* egg bagels
thinly sliced red onion, tomato, and lettuce leaves

Separate the egg yolks and whites. Chop the whites and crumble the yolks. Place in a bowl with onion, mayonnaise, tarragon or basil, salt, and pepper. Lightly mix and mash with a fork, and adjust seasonings. Spread on bagels, toasted or not, and top with onion, lettuce, and tomato. Store leftovers in the refrigerator.

MAKES 2 SANDWICHES

"There was a time when every Jewish housewife cherished her recipe for bagels. But today such excellent ones are had in the bakeries that they are rarely baked at home."

> —*from* The Jewish Festival Cookbook *by Fannie Engle and Gertrude Blair*

CHICKEN SALAD SANDWICH

2 boneless chicken breast halves
chicken stock *or* water to cover
1 Granny Smith apple, peeled, cored,
    and diced
1 celery rib, diced
1½ teaspoons capers, drained
¼ cup mayonnaise
2 tablespoons Dijon mustard
salt and freshly ground black pepper
lemon juice to taste
2 bagels, toasted
thinly sliced red onion, tomato, and
    lettuce leaves

Place the chicken breasts in a medium pot. Add stock or water to cover. Bring to a simmer, and cook, uncovered, 20 minutes. Remove chicken to cool. When cool enough to handle, remove and discard the skin. Cut the chicken into large chunks and place in a bowl.

Add the remaining ingredients and gently combine. Adjust seasonings with salt, pepper, and lemon juice. Make sandwiches using bagels, onion, tomato, and lettuce to taste. Store leftovers in the refrigerator.

MAKES 2 SANDWICHES

CHOPPED LIVER SPREAD

This roughly chopped pâté, an American Jewish favorite for cocktail snacks and sandwiches, is surprisingly easy to make. Since the liver itself is so rich, it needs very little additional fat.

2 tablespoons butter
1 large onion, chopped
1 garlic clove, minced
1 pound chicken livers, fat trimmed
salt and freshly ground black pepper
2 hard-boiled eggs, peeled and quartered

Melt the butter in a medium skillet over medium heat. Sauté the onion and garlic until soft, about 5 minutes.

Pat the livers dry, and season generously with salt and pepper. Add to the pan, and sauté, stirring frequently, until brown all over and pink inside, 5 to 10 minutes. Transfer to a food processor along with the hard-boiled eggs. Process with short pulses until a coarse paste is formed. Transfer to crock, and chill.

Serve cold or room temperature, open-faced on toasted bagels, with thinly sliced onion, radishes, and black olives. Chopped liver is, of course, delicious dabbed on crackers or toast points.

MAKES 1½ CUPS, ENOUGH FOR 6 SANDWICHES

The Great Bagel Controversy

Forget plain versus egg, these days the bagel is mired in even more dire controversy. Its very nature is being challenged by the boiling versus steaming controversy. What it boils down to is this: In the old-fashioned method, bagels were boiled briefly to tighten the skin, eliminate expansion, and give the crust its shine. Contemporary bagel-makers have worked a shortcut around this two-step process by injecting steam into the ovens as the bagels bake, thereby eliminating boiling. Steam causes the dough to expand, resulting in a softer, airier bagel, and the crust never develops the snap of a boiled bagel. A steamed bagel is, essentially, a less challenging eating experience, but it's the one most of us are settling for these days. As Jewish baker and bagel aficionado Izzy Cohen says, "Taste is a personal thing." But try his recipe on page 12 for the true, chewy thing.

FARMER BAGEL

Farmer cheese, sold in the supermarket, is a mild, fresh-tasting, light cheese that is great for spreading.

bagel
butter for spreading
farmer cheese
freshly ground black pepper

Cut open and toast the bagel, if desired. Lightly coat with butter, and then spread each side with about 2 tablespoons farmer cheese. Sprinkle with pepper and serve.

MAKES 1 SANDWICH

SMOKED WHITEFISH SALAD

This Jewish delicacy is available in bagel special-ty shops and good Jewish delis. It is also deli-cious spread on a toasted, buttered bialy.

plain, onion, *or* garlic bagel
butter for spreading
4 ounces smoked whitefish salad
thinly sliced red onion, tomato, and
    lettuce leaves

Split the bagel, and toast, if desired. Lightly spread with butter, and spread each half with whitefish. Top with garnish as desired and serve open-faced.

MAKES 1 SANDWICH

PEANUT BUTTER, JELLY, AND BANANA SANDWICH

It takes an energetic child with a strong jaw to chow down on this hunk o' culinary love.

plain bagel, preferably small and soft
peanut butter
strawberry *or* raspberry jelly
medium banana slices

Lightly coat untoasted bagel with peanut butter on one side and jelly on the other. Top the peanut butter with a single layer of medium-thick banana slices. Close sandwich and cut in half.

MAKES 1 SANDWICH

BIRTHDAY BAGEL

What a great birthday breakfast for any childlike gourmets in the house (a candle for making a wish is optional) or a logical choice for a toddler's interactive buffet. Nutella, a chocolate hazelnut spread from Europe, is available in gourmet markets and in the jam and jellies section of some supermarkets.

miniature plain or chocolate chip bagels
nutella spread
miniature marshmallows, toasted chopped
    walnuts or pecans, and miniature M&Ms®
    for garnish

Slice the bagels open and spread each with a thin layer of nutella. Have the children decorate according to taste with marshmallows, nuts, and miniature M&Ms®.

MAKES 1 SANDWICH

CUTTING-EDGE
SPREADS

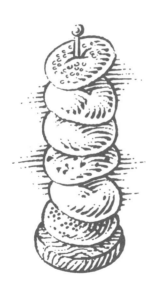

EGGPLANT CAVIAR

This garlicky spread is excellent as a dip with bagel chips or on a plain or garlic bagel sandwich along with a thinly sliced, grilled piece of chicken breast and a few peppery greens.

2 medium eggplants, trimmed
olive oil for coating
salt and freshly ground black pepper
5 garlic cloves, peeled
2 tablespoons olive oil
3 tablespoons lemon juice
½ medium onion, chopped

Preheat oven to 450 degrees F. Cut eggplants in half lengthwise, and score in criss-cross pattern. Rub all over with olive oil, sprinkle with salt and pepper, and bake, cut-sides up, about 1 hour, until soft. When cool enough to handle, scrape out pulp, and roughly chop.

With food processor on, add garlic to mince. Add eggplant, olive oil, and lemon juice, and purée until smooth. Season to taste with salt and pepper, and pulse to combine. Transfer to mixing bowl, stir in onions, and serve at room temperature or chilled.

ENOUGH FOR 6 SERVINGS

WHITE BEAN GARLIC SPREAD

Mashed beans and garlic make a wonderful, hearty spread.

3 tablespoons olive oil
2 garlic cloves, minced
1 (15-ounce) can cannelini *or* white beans,
   drained and rinsed
salt and freshly ground black pepper
lemon juice to taste

Heat the olive oil in a small skillet over medium-low heat. Sauté the garlic until soft, about 5 minutes. Add the beans, salt, and pepper, and cook, stirring and mashing with a fork, until a paste is formed, about 10 minutes. Adjust seasonings with salt, pepper, and lemon juice. Serve warm or at room temperature on toasted plain, garlic, or onion bagel halves. Top with arugula or black olives.

MAKES 1 CUP, 2 SERVINGS

A Bagel Time Line

1610—Bagels receive their first mention in print in the official Community Relations code of Kraków, Poland. Citizens are advised to give bagels to women in childbirth. In modern Kraków, bagels are still sold as street food.

1683—Polish general Jan Sobieski introduces the bagel to jubilant Austrians while defeating the invading Turks. The citizens of Vienna cling to his stirrups, or buegels, and famed Viennese bakers bake (what else?) bagels in his honor.

1907—International Beigel Bakers Union, local 338, founded in New York, for the protection and improvement of approximately 300 specialty bakers working in about 36 union bagel shops in the New York metropolitan area.

1927—*Harry Lender, a baker from Lublin, Poland, starts his bagel bakery in New Haven, Connecticut.*

1947—*Western Bagel opens in the Van Nuys neighborhood of Los Angeles, introducing the professionally baked bagel to previously deprived West Coast Jews.*

1951—*The Broadway show* Bagels and Yox *promotes the bagel concept and Jewish humor to a receptive New York audience.*

1962—*Bagel machine invented by Dan Thompson, boosting production to 400 dozen an hour.*

1962—*Harry's son, Murray Lender, begins mass distribution of frozen bagels—one of the fastest-growing items in today's grocery freezer case.*

1971—*John Marx, of Marx Hot Bagel Factory in Cincinnati, dons blue tights, shorts, and a cape to become the first bagel superhero, even-*

tually leading to a plug by Charles Kurault on national television.

1984—*Lender's Bagels is sold to Kraft, Inc., for $60 million.*

1996—*Annual bagel sales shoot to $2.6 billion; stock in bagel specialty stores is publicly traded; California-based Noah's introduces the cross-cultural gingerbread bagel for Thanksgiving; and a bagel shop finally opens in Wyoming.*

TAPENADE

Serve lusty homemade olive spread on toasted baguette slices, as part of an updated tuna sandwich (see page 52) or as a dip with bagel chips.

1 cup Kalamata olives, pitted
1 tablespoon drained capers
1 garlic clove
juice of 1 lemon
6 tablespoons good-quality olive oil
6 sprigs thyme, leaves only

Place all of the ingredients in the bowl of a food processor or blender, and process until a chunky paste is formed. Store in a sealed container in the refrigerator.

MAKES ½ CUP

HUMMUS

*This Middle Eastern garbanzo bean spread can
be served alone on a bagel with thinly sliced red
onion and olives, or in a sandwich with some
roasted eggplant slices or grilled chicken breast.*

1 (15-ounce) can chick peas (garbanzo
beans)
3 tablespoons tahini paste (sesame seed
paste)
3 garlic cloves, minced
2 tablespoons lemon juice
2 tablespoons olive oil
salt and freshly ground black pepper, to
taste
paprika and additional olive oil for garnish

Empty the chick peas with canning liquid (or drain and add ¼ cup water) into food processor or blender. Add tahini, garlic, lemon juice, and olive oil, and purée until a smooth paste is formed. Season to taste with salt and pepper, and process briefly. Transfer to a serving bowl or container. Sprinkle with paprika, and drizzle a little olive oil over the top. Store in the refrigerator.

ENOUGH FOR 3 SANDWICHES

"Bagels have gotten too big and pouffy. All that soft dough in the middle you could take out and use for cleaning wallpaper."

> —*Mimi Sheraton, food writer and former* New York Times *restaurant critic*

WILD MUSHROOM SPREAD

Serve this rich spread open-faced on plain or garlic bagels for a sumptuous veggie bagel.

4 tablespoons butter
½ cup chopped shallots
2 garlic cloves, minced
6 ounces shiitake mushroom caps, chopped
12 ounces cremini mushrooms, chopped
salt and freshly ground pepper
2 tablespoons cognac *or* brandy
2 tablespoons chopped fresh herbs such as
    parsley, thyme, *or* tarragon
3 tablespoons heavy cream
½ cup pecan halves, toasted
juice of 1 lemon

Melt butter in large skillet over medium heat. Sauté shallots and garlic until soft, 5 minutes. Add mushrooms, salt, and pepper. Turn heat to high, and cook, stirring frequently, until mushrooms cook down and release their liquid.

Add cognac or brandy and herbs, and continue cooking until liquid evaporates. Pour in cream, and boil until pan is nearly dry. Transfer to food processor along with nuts, and pulse until a chunky spread is formed. Season with lemon juice, salt, and pepper. Mix to combine, and transfer to a crock. Chill or serve at room temperature.

MAKES 2 CUPS, ENOUGH FOR 8 SANDWICHES

How to Store a Bagel

Fresh bagels can be stored in a brown paper bag at room temperature for a day. Store those you don't plan on eating the first day in a plastic bag in the freezer, and split them before freezing for quicker eating—these can go directly from freezer to toaster. If you don't split them first, defrost for about 15 minutes at room temperature, or defrost in a 350-degree oven about 5 minutes before toasting. Never microwave a bagel—they're supposed to be tough, but not that tough.

TOFU SCALLION MASH

If it is substitute cream cheese you are after, Tofutti makes a very good product. This topping is more along the lines of a coarsely mashed savory spread for bagels, crackers, or crudités.

1 (10.5-ounce) package firm tofu
5 scallions, white and half green, chopped
1 small garlic clove, minced
1 bunch fresh chives, chopped
2 tablespoons olive oil
1 tablespoon lemon juice
salt and freshly ground black pepper

Roughly chop the tofu, and place in a bowl. Add the remaining ingredients, and mash with a fork to desired consistency.

ENOUGH FOR 3 SANDWICHES

AVOCADO PEPPER MASH

Guacamole, by another name, is terrific all by itself or as a spread on a roasted turkey sandwich.

2 ripe Haas avocados, peeled and seeded
1 jalapeño *or* serrano pepper, seeded and
   minced
3 tablespoons red onion, minced
juice of 1 lime
salt and Tabasco to taste

Roughly chop the avocados, and place in a bowl. Add remaining ingredients, and mash with a fork to desired consistency. Adjust seasonings with salt, Tabasco, and lime. Store in the refrigerator.

ENOUGH FOR 3 SANDWICHES

GRIDDLED
SANDWICHES

SALAMI AND EGGS

*For those times when low fat just won't do—
a nice, hot sandwich of garlicky salami and eggs.
Serve with a chocolate egg cream for a totally
retro, hi-cal lunch.*

1 tablespoon butter
4 thin slices kosher salami, preferably
    hand-cut, cut in quarters
2 eggs
1 or 2 tablespoons milk
salt, freshly ground pepper, and Tabasco
1 plain, garlic, *or* onion bagel, split and
    toasted

Melt the butter in a small skillet over low heat. Fry the salami until lightly browned on both sides.

Meanwhile beat together the eggs, milk, salt, pepper, and Tabasco. Pour into pan and raise heat to medium. Cook, lifting edges and swirling pan to set evenly. When puffed and nearly done, flip with spatula to finish. Turn out onto uncoated, toasted bagel. Close with top half, cut in half, and serve hot.

MAKES 1

Bagel Destinations
The best states for traveling bagel lovers are New York, New Jersey, California, Pennsylvania, and Florida—with the highest concentrations of bagel retail shops. States to be avoided are West Virginia and Mississippi, where, as of 1996, bagel shops did not exist.

FRIED HAM AND EGG SANDWICH

It may not be kosher, but ham with eggs on a bagel does make an excellent sandwich.

1 bagel, split
butter
3 slices Canadian bacon
1 egg
freshly ground black pepper

Toast and butter a bagel. Place on plate.

In a small skillet, melt about a teaspoon of butter over medium heat. Fry the ham until lightly browned along the edges, 1 or 2 minutes per side. Place on bagel half to cover.

Crack the egg into same skillet, and reduce heat to low. Fry until white is nearly set. Flip (don't worry about breaking), and cook just to set, less than 1 minute. Top ham with egg, and sprinkle generously with pepper. Press on top half of bagel, and cut in half. The yolk will spill and make a messy but delicious puddle for dipping.

MAKES 1

GRILLED CHEESE AND TOMATO

Beware of garlic and onion when choosing a bagel for toasting under the broiler. Burnt garlic chips can ruin an otherwise pleasant eating experience.

1 bagel, split
butter and mustard for spreading
Gruyere, Swiss, *or* cheddar cheese,
    thinly sliced
tomato, thinly sliced
bacon slices, crisp-cooked (optional)

Lightly toast the bagel, and lightly coat with butter and mustard. Top both halves with cheese slices to cover and a single layer of tomato. In a toaster oven or under the broiler, cook just to melt the cheese, being careful not to burn. Serve open-faced, topped with bacon slices, if desired.

MAKES 1

PIZZA BAGEL

Fusion cooking at its simplest—a Jewish-Italian-American childhood favorite.

> 2 plain or garlic bagels
> ¼ cup prepared tomato sauce
> 6 tablespoons shredded mozzarella cheese
> 3 slices pepperoni, quartered (optional)

Split the bagels, and lightly toast. Spread with a thin layer of tomato sauce. Sprinkle on the cheese, and top with pepperoni, if desired. In a toaster oven or under the broiler, cook just to melt the cheese, being careful not to burn. Serve hot and open-faced.

MAKES 2

GRIDDLED PORTOBELLO BAGELS

A sandwich for the '90s—marinated mushroom and bitter greens piled on a toasted (or grilled) bagel.

1 portobello mushroom cap, wiped clean
¼ cup olive oil
1 garlic clove, minced
1 tablespoon chopped fresh parsley, thyme,
    or marjoram
salt and freshly ground black pepper
2 plain or garlic bagels, lightly toasted
olive oil for brushing
4 sprigs arugula *or* watercress

Place the mushroom in a bowl. Add the oil, garlic, and fresh herbs. Turn the mushroom to coat evenly, and marinate at room temperature ½ to 2 hours.

Preheat the broiler or a grill pan over high heat. Broil or pan-grill the mushroom until slightly charred on the edges, about 2 minutes per side. Cut the mushroom in half, and season with salt and pepper.

Lightly brush toasted bagels with olive oil. Place mushroom halves on bottoms, top with greens, and close to make sandwiches.

MAKES 2

TUNA BAGEL MELT

2 bagels
butter for spreading
tuna salad (see page 52)
1 tablespoon mustard
1 tablespoon chopped fresh dill
thinly sliced Gruyere, Swiss, *or*
    cheddar cheese
2 tomato slices (optional)

Split the bagels, lightly toast, and spread with butter.

In a bowl, mash together tuna salad, mustard, and dill. Top each bagel half with a cheese slice. Spread a layer of tuna on two halves (on top of the cheese). Place all 4 halves on a baking sheet or a toaster oven pan. Bake in oven at 425 degrees F or brown the tops in a toaster oven until cheese melts and tuna bubbles.

Carefully transfer to plates. Top each tuna half with an optional tomato slice and top with the cheese half. Press together, cut in half, and serve warm.

SERVES 2

CONVERSIONS

LIQUID
1 Tbsp = 15 ml
½ cup = 4 fl oz = 125 ml
1 cup = 8 fl oz = 250 ml

DRY
¼ cup = 4 Tbsp = 2 oz = 60 g
1 cup = ½ pound = 8 oz = 250 g

FLOUR
½ cup = 60 g
1 cup = 4 oz = 125 g

TEMPERATURE
400° F = 200° C = gas mark 6
375° F = 190° C = gas mark 5
350° F = 175° C = gas mark 4

MISCELLANEOUS
2 Tbsp butter = 1 oz = 30 g
1 inch = 2.5 cm
all-purpose flour = plain flour
baking soda = bicarbonate of soda
brown sugar = demerara sugar
confectioners' sugar = icing sugar
heavy cream = double cream
molasses = black treacle
raisins = sultanas
rolled oats = oat flakes
semisweet chocolate = plain chocolate
sugar = caster sugar